AIRCRAFT

Rescue Helicopters and Aircraft

Henry M. Holden

Enslow Publishers, Inc.

40 Industrial Road   PO Box 38
Box 398   Aldershot
Berkeley Heights, NJ 07922   Hants GU12 6BP
USA   UK

http://www.enslow.com

Library of Congress Cataloging-in-Publication Data

Holden, Henry M.
    Rescue helicopters and aircraft / Henry M. Holden.
       p. cm. — (Aircraft)
    Includes bibliographical references and index.
    Summary: Presents firsthand accounts of real-life rescues, and examines
pilot training, aircraft specifications, and specialized equipment used in air
rescue operations.
    ISBN 0-7660-1719-2
       1. Aeronautics—Relief service—Juvenile literature. 2.Helicopters—
Juvenile literature. 3. Airplanes—Juvenile literature. 4. Rescue work—Juvenile
literature. [1. Helicopters. 2. Airplanes. 3.Rescue work.] I. Title. II. Aircraft
(Berkeley Heights, N.J.)
    TL722.8 .H65 2002
    629.133'352—dc21

                  2001006717

Printed in the United States of America

10 9 8 7 6 5 4 3 2 1

To Our Readers: We have done our best to make sure all Internet Addresses in this
book were active and appropriate when we went to press. However, the author and
the publisher have no control over and assume no liability for the material avail-
able on those Internet sites or on other Web sites they may link to. Any comments
or suggestions can be sent by e-mail to comments@enslow.com or to the address
on the back cover.

Photo Credits: Cessna Aircraft Corporation, p. 26; © Corel Corporation, pp. 3, 10, 17,
29, 35; Department of Defense, pp. 4–5, 12, 14, 16, 38, 40; Enslow Publishers, Inc.,
pp. 8, 37; Henry M. Holden, pp. 33, 39; NASA, p. 32; U.S. Air Force, p. 7; U.S. Coast
Guard, pp. 18, 20, 21, 23, 27; U.S. Customs Service, p. 31; U.S. Marine Corps, p. 13.

Cover Photo: Department of Defense (U.S. Marine Super Stallion helicopter)

Contents

CHAPTER 1

Pilot Down

F-16 Fighters

It was June 2, 1995. Two F-16 fighter jets were flying a standard "two-ship" formation. Air Force Captain Bob "Wilbur" Wright was the lead pilot. Captain Scott O'Grady was his wingman, making sure enemy fighters did not sneak up behind Wright. The Serbians,

Bosnian Muslims, and Croatians were fighting in Bosnia (known as Bosnia and Herzegovina). The pilots' mission was to keep all unfriendly planes out of the sky. This was O'Grady's forty-seventh mission over Bosnia. That day his call sign was Basher Five-Two. Wright was Basher Five-One.

≡ Radar Contact

Wright and O'Grady were 27,000 feet high, speeding through the air at 500 miles per hour. Suddenly O'Grady's threat-warning alarm sounded. He scanned the skies for the telltale trail of white smoke from a surface-to-air missile, the only visual clue a pilot has that a missile is heading toward him. Once the missile burns up its fuel, it cannot be seen with the naked eye. It travels at twice the speed of sound.

O'Grady could see nothing. A second later the sky exploded in front of him. A Bosnian Serb missile had passed between the two airplanes and exploded harmlessly. However, O'Grady knew surface-to-air missiles were fired in pairs. A second one was in the air. O'Grady thought about escape maneuvers, but he was too late.

≡ Bail Out

"Then came a blow like nothing I had ever felt," said O'Grady. "It was like getting rear-ended by a speeding eighteen-wheeler with a [rocket] strapped to its hood."[1]

The missile had struck one of O'Grady's fuel tanks and cut the F-16 in two. Flames burst into the cockpit and surrounded him. O'Grady could feel the heat through his oxygen mask. The airplane was falling apart around him. Any second the airplane would explode. He reached for the fat yellow handle attached to his seat. Even through the flames, he could see the words *Pull to Eject* on the ejection seat handle. He pulled with all his strength.

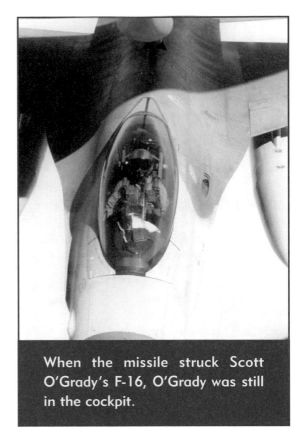

When the missile struck Scott O'Grady's F-16, O'Grady was still in the cockpit.

A split second later, the seat rocketed O'Grady into the sky at nearly 500 miles an hour. He was clear of the flaming airplane, but his troubles were only beginning. He was five miles above Earth and falling like a rock. His parachute would automatically open at 14,000 feet, but he could not wait. He pulled the handle that opened the parachute. He heard a pop as the parachute opened. He was still strapped in his seat.

At 24,000 feet, the oxygen was thin. The parachute had slowed his descent to about 1,000 feet a minute. It would take almost a half hour for him to reach the ground. This was a problem, since he was over enemy territory. The parachute would be spotted long before he'd have a chance to land. At 14,000 feet, the seat automatically fell away. By then O'Grady could see farmland and vehicles below.

As O'Grady looked down during his drop, he saw a military truck with a canvas back. People on the ground could watch him. "They were standing there waiting for me the whole time," said O'Grady.[2]

O'Grady landed off the road. He removed his chute and ran for the cover of some trees. He heard footsteps and voices just five feet from his hiding place. Several local villagers, not soldiers, stood looking around. They all had guns.

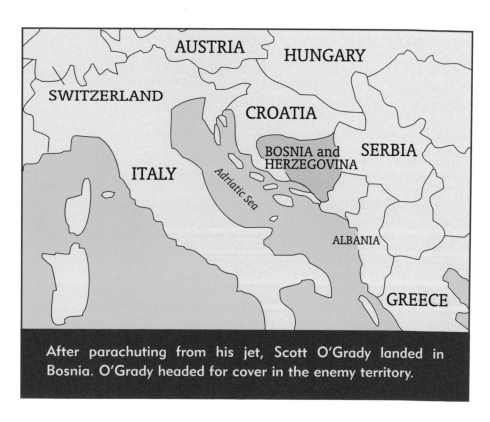

After parachuting from his jet, Scott O'Grady landed in Bosnia. O'Grady headed for cover in the enemy territory.

Suddenly, O'Grady heard one gunshot, then another. There was more scattered gunfire. The villagers did not know exactly where O'Grady was hiding. "I hunkered down," he said, "afraid that my heart would explode in my chest. . . . I didn't think I'd ever make it back to my family and friends again."[3]

O'Grady waited until after midnight to make his move. He had three goals: to survive, to evade the enemy, and to make radio contact. He had some food, water, a radio, a pistol, and a Global Positioning System (GPS) receiver.

The GPS uses signals from some of the 24 satellites that are 12,500 miles out in space. The GPS receiver would tell him his exact location. Both the radio and GPS receiver worked on batteries. He did not know how long the batteries would last or how long it would be before he was rescued. He called on his radio several times over the next few days. All he heard was static.

CHAPTER 2

Rescued from the Enemy

By the time Scott O'Grady had been on the ground for six days, he was cold, hungry, and exhausted, but he would not give up. He had successfully evaded the enemy, but had run out of food and water. He was surviving on grass, leaves, and ants.[1] One night it had rained, and he had faced the sky to drink in the raindrops. He even managed to collect about a pint of rainwater in a resealable plastic bag for later use.

He did not know it, but the U.S. Air Force had picked up his radio signals, and Wright had been looking for him. At 2:08 A.M. on the sixth day, O'Grady heard eight wonderful words over his radio: "Basher

Five-Two, read you loud and clear." Through a code word, Wright determined that it really was Scott O'Grady at the other end of the radio transmission.

A call went out to the U.S. Marine Corps' forty-two-member Tactical Recovery Aircraft and Personnel, or TRAP, force. This team rescues downed pilots behind enemy lines. They were on the USS *Kearsarge*, an aircraft carrier in the Adriatic Sea, and would fly by helicopter to rescue O'Grady.

The next morning, two Marine Corps CH-53E Super Stallion helicopters took off from the carrier. They were carrying Marines to help rescue O'Grady. Two AH-1T Sea Cobra helicopter gunships followed them. A dozen other fighter planes would fly air cover on this rescue mission. They would make sure enemy fighters did not jump the rescue party.

It was a little after 6:00 A.M. when one of the Marine pilots radioed O'Grady. "He promised that the rescue choppers would be there within thirty minutes. That half hour was the longest in my life," said O'Grady.[2]

O'Grady hid behind some trees in the woods. He hoped the enemy was far away. First, the Cobra gunships came in. They flew over the area looking for enemy soldiers. When they did not see any, they hovered over a spot near O'Grady. "The pilot of the first chopper radioed for me to 'pop smoke,'" said O'Grady.[3]

O'Grady set off one of his red phosphorus flares. This signaled Marine choppers as to his exact location.

A U.S. Marine Corps Super Stallion was used to lead the rescue of Captain Scott O'Grady.

However, it would also alert the enemy that he was in the area.

The Cobras remained hovering in the air near the landing zone, watching for enemy troops. Their job was to keep the enemy from getting near O'Grady and to make sure it was safe for the Marine Super Stallion helicopters to land. Above the Cobras were British Harrier jump jets. They were watching for enemy fighter planes in the sky.

The Super Stallion helicopters came in fast. The downdraft from their rotor blades kicked up clouds of dirt, dust, and grass as they landed. Before the helicopters had their wheels on the ground, the Marines were jumping off and fanning out across the hilltop. They were dressed in battle gear: bulletproof vests, helmets, and goggles to protect their eyes from the swirling dirt around them. Either standing or kneeling, they pointed their M-16 assault weapons in all directions to form a defense in case any enemy troops showed up. They would hold that position until O'Grady was safely on board the helicopter. Meanwhile, the Super Stallions did not shut down their engines, and the Cobra gunships continued to hover and watch for enemy troops.

O'Grady started running for the first helicopter. He was zigzagging through the woods toward the landing zone. He had his pistol in his right hand and his radio in his left. He tripped on some vines and fell. The Cobra pilot

Cobra helicopters, like the ones shown here, watched for the enemy as Scott O'Grady ran to safety.

shouted to him over the radio to get up and keep running. The pilot was sure the enemy had heard the noise of the helicopters and was on the way to O'Grady's location.

When O'Grady reached the helicopter door, the crew chief tapped him on the wrist. O'Grady still had the gun in his hand. It would be dangerous inside the helicopter. O'Grady might accidentally fire it. O'Grady dropped the gun and climbed aboard. With O'Grady safely on the

U.S. Air Force Captains T. O. Hanford (left), Scott O'Grady (center), and Bob Wright (right) speak at a press conference. After six days of evading the enemy, O'Grady was rescued by the U.S. Marines. Captain Hanford made the first radio contact with O'Grady before his rescue and Captain Wright was O'Grady's lead pilot.

helicopter, the Marines scrambled back onboard the Super Stallions.

The helicopters were ready to take off. The pilot pushed forward the throttles of the three powerful jet engines. The seventy-nine-foot rotor was whirling in a blur.

Six minutes after the Super Stallions landed, they were lifting off under full power with Scott O'Grady on one of them. He and the Marines were still not out of danger. As the helicopters flew west over Croatia toward the Adriatic Sea, Krajanian Serbs opened antiaircraft fire on them. A bullet cut through the main rotor of O'Grady's helicopter. A second damaged its tail rotor. A third hit the cabin and ricocheted into the canteen of one of the Marines. The door gunner returned the fire as the choppers scrambled for the safety of the Adriatic Sea. The pilot took the helicopter down to treetop level to evade further ground fire. By 7:15 A.M., they were clear of enemy airspace, and they were safe.

Specifications for
CH-53E Super Stallion

Height—28 feet 4 inches

Length—99 feet ½ inch

Main rotor diameter—79 feet

Engines—3

Crew—3 and up to 55 troops

Maximum speed—195 miles per hour

Cruise speed—172 miles per hour

Range—1,290 miles

CHAPTER 3

Lifeguard Flights and Rescue Aircraft

Helicopters and fixed-wing aircraft also rescue civilians who have been stranded by floods or hurricanes. They also fly sick or injured people to hospitals. Sometimes these flights are called lifeguard flights.

Helicopters are often used to rescue people in cases where they would be faster than an ambulance. They can hover—fly without moving in any direction—and land in tight areas such as on roads or on the rooftops of some hospitals. They can fly over roads that are blocked and rescue people stranded by storms or other disasters.

Helicopters that fly critically ill or injured people to hospitals are called

The Jayhawk can land on the roof of a hospital. Emergency technicians can then rush the patient to the emergency room.

medevac helicopters. *Medevac* is short for "*med*ical *evac*uation." These helicopters sometimes have the radio call sign "Lifeguard." The call sign Lifeguard informs air traffic controllers that the helicopter is on a medical emergency. Lifeguard flights get special permission to fly through areas with heavy air traffic.[1]

Medevac missions are sometimes dangerous. The pilots may have to fly through storms and into areas where radio towers and other obstacles can be dangerous to aircraft.

Medevac pilots are trained to take off within about eight minutes of notification. They are able to do this by having their helicopters on standby. They start the engines at the beginning of each day to make sure they are working properly. The pilots call this a run-up. The crew also keeps its medical equipment in place in the helicopter.

≡ Rescue Helicopters

Rescue helicopters come in many different sizes. One of the largest is the Black Hawk helicopter. This military aircraft is often used during civilian emergencies. The Air National Guard, U.S. Coast Guard, and U.S. Customs Service use it to evacuate hurricane and flood victims when the roads are unusable. It flies people to hospitals, and it delivers food, water, and medical supplies to help victims in these areas.

Four whirling blades make up the 54-foot main rotor on the top of the helicopter. Each blade is made of fiberglass with a titanium edge. The blades are filled with nitrogen gas.[2] This makes them very light and strong. The helicopter can fly as fast as 200 miles per hour. With its additional fuel tanks, the Black Hawk can travel about 700 miles before it needs refueling.

The Coast Guard version of the Black Hawk helicopter is called the Jayhawk. The U.S. Coast Guard uses the Jayhawk on medevac missions and to rescue people who are on damaged boats.

On September 2, 1998, Hurricane Earl was smashing into the Florida city of Destin, on the Gulf of Mexico. The Coast Guard air station at Mobile, Alabama, got a call that two fishing boats were in trouble in the water. The wind in the area was reported to be ninety miles per hour.

The U.S. Coast Guard launched an HH-60 Jayhawk helicopter. En route to Destin, it joined up with a Coast Guard HU-25 FalconJet. The jet cannot land on water, but it can get to the victims faster than the Jayhawk. It could drop a datum marker buoy, a device that would transmit an electronic signal from the location of the boats.

Just south of Pensacola, the FalconJet radioed that it could not penetrate the hurricane because of the severe turbulence and a radar failure on board the aircraft.

The Jayhawk continued into the storm. As it got closer to Destin, the crew heard an emergency radio signal from one of the boats. They used their radio-direction-finding equipment to follow the signal. At last the pilots saw a flashing emergency light and two people sitting on top of an overturned boat.

The Coast Guard calls the Black Hawk helicopter the Jayhawk. During a search and rescue mission, the pilots look for small boats in the ocean.

Specifications for
HH-60 Jayhawk

Height—16 feet 10 inches

Length—64 feet 10 inches

Main rotor diameter—53 feet

Engines—2

Crew—4

Maximum speed—206 miles per hour

Cruise speed—161 miles per hour

Endurance—4½ miles

Range—800 miles

Maximum altitude—5,000 feet

A rescue swimmer onboard the helicopter was lowered into the gigantic waves to help the two men into the rescue basket, one at a time. The high wind, towering seas, and driving rain made the rescue dangerous. But the rescue was successful.

The helicopter crew began to look for the other boat and possible survivors there. Using night-vision goggles, they soon discovered a man in the water and debris from the second boat. Again the rescue swimmer jumped into the water and helped the victim into the basket. The crew continued to search for the other man until they ran low on fuel.

The helicopter flew to nearby Eglin Air Force Base, where it dropped off the survivors and refueled. It then flew back into the hurricane to search for the missing man. For over eight hours, the team searched in winds of about sixty-eight miles per hour and blinding rain. They could not find him. They returned to base because they were again running low on fuel.[3]

Hercules to the Rescue

The U.S. Air Force and U.S. Coast Guard sometimes use the C-130 Hercules to help on rescue missions. This stubby-nosed, gigantic plane cannot land on the water, but it drops first aid supplies, food, and life rafts to people in the water. The U.S. Air Force also uses the Hercules as a flying ambulance. It can carry seventy-four stretcher patients and two medical attendants.

Specifications for
C-130 Hercules

Height—38 feet 3 inches

Length—97 feet 9 inches

Wingspan—132 feet 7 inches

Engines—4

Crew—About 5, depending on use

Maximum speed—About 400 miles per hour

Cruise speed—About 330 miles per hour

Endurance—About 14 to 16 hours

Range—About 2,800 miles

Maximum altitude—33,000 feet

The Air National Guard sometimes puts skis on the Hercules. It can then rescue people stranded in the snow. In October 2000, an LC-130 Hercules rescued Dr. Jerri Nielsen from the South Pole. She had cancer and needed an operation that could not be performed there. The temperature outside was ⁻58 degrees Fahrenheit. The Hercules could not stop its engines when it landed. It had only fifteen minutes to make the rescue before the airplane's landing gear would freeze up and the jet fuel would change to jelly.[4] The rescue was successful and Nielsen recovered from her surgery.

Rescue at Sea

Sometimes helicopters and fixed-wing aircraft work together to rescue people. On September 14, 1993, Captain John Mahoney was in his thirty-seven-foot fishing boat heading to Cape Cod Bay in Massachusetts. He was fishing for bait fish used by lobstermen.

Mahoney and two crew members had almost filled the nine-ton fish bin. His boat was getting heavy. Suddenly, the wall of the fish hold broke and the fish spilled out. Waves began coming over the back of the boat.

Mahoney was in trouble. He got on his radio. "Mayday! Mayday!" he called.[5]

Omaha 13 heard his distress call. Omaha 13 was the call sign of a U.S. Customs Service fixed-wing Piper Navajo. The crew asked Mahoney for his position.

Mahoney told them his location. When Customs pilots Cris Baur and Mike Brenner heard the position, they realized that they were near the fishing boat. They called the U.S. Coast Guard.

"We were only eight minutes away," said Baur. The U.S. Coast Guard asked the pilots to fly over the scene, since the Jayhawk helicopter was still twenty minutes away.

Baur and Brenner pushed the twin engine's throttles to get the maximum speed possible. Mahoney's anxious voice came across the radio again. "We're going down fast!"

The temperature of the water was a chilly sixty degrees Fahrenheit. Wind gusts were whipping up six-foot waves. The fishermen would die if they were not rescued quickly.

When the pilots arrived over the scene, they found an oil slick and some debris. They also saw three men in the water. Most Customs aircraft operating over water carry a survival raft. Omaha 13 had a five-man raft on board.

To get the raft to the fishermen, who had been in the water just a few minutes, Brenner had to open the airplane door and push it out. He had to make sure he did not fall out of the plane when he pushed it. He needed to drop the raft as close to the men as possible without dropping it on them. The six-foot seas would make it very difficult for them to swim to the raft. On the other hand, the forty-pound life raft could kill a man instantly if it hit him. The raft fell toward the three men at almost one hundred miles per hour.

"All I saw were three heads whiz by!" said Brenner when the raft left his hands.[6] The Customs pilots flew over once more. The men in the water had gotten into the raft.

The Coast Guard's Jayhawk helicopter arrived about fifteen minutes later. They lifted the fishermen from the raft and flew them to the hospital. All three men recovered. Eventually Mahoney even salvaged his boat from a depth of seventy-five feet.

Flying with Angels

There are times when seriously ill people need fast transportation to a hospital. Also, human blood and organs sometimes need to be rushed to a hospital when a patient is awaiting a transplant operation. "Angel" flights can play a big role in these situations.

The Cessna CJ2 may be used for angel flights. It can land at small airports, which may be close to a needed hospital.

Specifications for
HU-25 Guardian FalconJet

Height—18 feet

Length—56 feet

Wingspan—54 feet

Engines—2

Crew—5

Maximum speed—517 miles per hour

Cruise speed—471 miles per hour

Endurance—4½ hours

Range—About 2,000 miles

Maximum altitude—42,000 feet

Sometimes corporations donate empty seats on their jets to patients in need of treatment. These corporate angel flights avoid commercial airport delays and can take a patient to a treatment facility quickly. One of the airplanes used for angel flights is the Cessna CJ2. This airplane can fly 45,000 feet high at 300 miles per hour. It can carry up to six people.

≡ *Teamwork*

In July 2001, a single-engine Cessna Caravan transmitted a Mayday shortly after leaving Freeport, in the Bahamas. The crew said they were going down in the ocean. An air traffic controller in the Miami Air Route Traffic Control Center heard the call and sent another aircraft to try to locate the Caravan before it went down. Next, he contacted a Coast Guard FalconJet and sent it to meet the airplane. The FalconJet dropped a life raft into the shark-infested water. A Coast Guard helicopter was also on its way to the crash site. The two men aboard the Caravan, who crashed into the water about thirty miles off Fort Lauderdale, Florida, were rescued about three minutes later.[7]

CHAPTER 4

Medevac Equipment and Crew Training

There was no moon in the sky, and a thick fog was rolling across the highway. The driver of a sport utility vehicle (SUV) was behind a shiny aluminum eighteen-wheeler. The SUV's headlights were reflecting off the trailer. The light was blinding the driver, so he decided to pass the truck.

The driver stepped on the gas, then pulled out to pass. Suddenly, headlights appeared in the oncoming lane. The driver of the SUV slammed on the brakes and swerved off the road. The squealing tires gave way to the crunch of steel. The SUV rolled over in a ditch and came to rest upside down. Several other drivers pulled off the road and stopped. One called 911 on his cell phone.

Ten minutes later, an ambulance arrived. The emergency medical technician (EMT) examined the driver and found he was seriously injured. He needed a medevac helicopter.[1]

≡ Tools for the Rescue

A medevac helicopter is a flying emergency room and ambulance all in one. It carries a pilot, flight nurse, and flight paramedic. It also carries medical equipment such as oxygen, bandages, IV bottles, heart medications, and painkillers. Some helicopters have medical equipment such as EKGs to record heart rhythm, and heart defibrillators.

Within minutes of the call from the EMT, a Eurocopter BK-117 medevac helicopter was in the air. The BK-117 can carry two pilots, two injured persons, a flight nurse, and a flight paramedic.

Ten minutes after the EMT made the call, the rescue helicopter touched down on the highway. The flight nurse examined the man's injuries. He had serious head injuries and internal bleeding. They needed to get him to a hospital quickly if he was to survive. The faster a victim reaches the hospital, the better his chance for survival. A thirty-mile ambulance ride may take forty-five minutes, depending on traffic. A helicopter can cover that distance in about fifteen minutes.

One way rescue helicopter pilots see at night is with a bright searchlight. Their searchlights have the intensity

Specifications for
Eurocopter BK-117

Height—11 feet 7 inches

Length—42 feet 7 inches

Main rotor diameter—72 feet

Engines—2

Crew—Up to 4, plus two injured persons

Maximum speed—153 miles per hour

Cruise speed—142 miles per hour

Range—260 miles

of 30 million candles. At night, the pilot needs one of these lights to find a safe landing zone.

Sometimes, when an injured person is lost in the mountains or in the ocean, rescuers first have to find the victim. If it is nighttime or if there is fog, a forward-looking infrared (FLIR) sensor allows the flight crew to see the person's body heat, even in total darkness. Things that are cold appear dark gray or black on the FLIR screen. Things that are warm appear light gray or white. A zoom lens helps operators tell humans from animals. Some infrared equipment can detect a 16-inch-wide hot spot from 8,000 feet away.[2]

All military rescue aircraft and many private aircraft use the Global Positioning System (GPS). If the pilot has the map location or coordinates of the victim, the GPS can guide the pilots to within a few feet of the victim. The GPS is a big help because a pilot cannot read street signs from 3,000 feet.

Night-vision goggles fit over the flight helmet and are worn by the flight crew when they are searching for someone at night. The person sees everything in a green glow like the color in this photo.

Water, trees, or other obstacles prevent helicopters from landing, so some helicopters have a rescue hoist with a basket. The hoist can lift injured people off the ground or out of the water. It can lift up to 600 pounds. The steel cable is about 250 feet long.

≡ Air Crew Training

Pilots who fly medevac choppers are highly trained and skilled. Bayflite Air Medical Transport, a medevac company in St. Petersburg, Florida, requires their pilots to have a commercial pilot's license with a helicopter instrument rating and at least 2,000 flight hours. Pilots

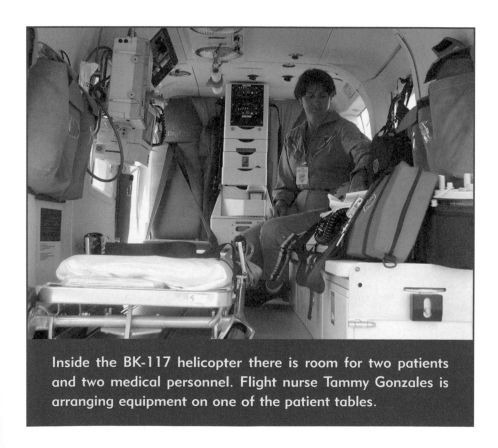

Inside the BK-117 helicopter there is room for two patients and two medical personnel. Flight nurse Tammy Gonzales is arranging equipment on one of the patient tables.

must have at least 250 hours of night flying and 250 hours of flying turbine-powered helicopters.[3]

"Bayflite has four helicopters," said flight nurse Tammy Gonzales. "We have them placed so one is never more than fifteen minutes from any area we cover."[4]

The flight nurse and flight paramedic always work as a team. They are flying emergency room personnel. They work long hours—sometimes twelve- or twenty-four-hour shifts—two or three times a week.[5]

Flight nurses must be registered nurses and they must pass a course to be certified for flight. Part of their training includes advanced cardiac life support and some basic surgical procedures. For example, they can open a person's neck and insert a tracheotomy tube to help the victim breathe if his mouth and nose are injured.[6]

Flight paramedics have special medical training. They usually have several years' experience as a paramedic on a ground ambulance. They are not doctors, but they can stop bleeding and administer intravenous fluids and some medications.

CHAPTER 5

Rescue in Alaska

At 5:00 P.M. on December 27, 1997, a man in a remote Alaskan village sustained a critical head injury. The village, on Akutan Island, part of the Aleutian Islands, is off the southwest coast of Alaska. The man had to be flown to a hospital or he would not live through the night.

The nearest Coast Guard air station was at Dutch Harbor, Alaska, but the aircraft there were grounded because of a snowstorm. The air station on Kodiak Island would have to answer the call. However, it was about six hundred miles away. It would be a long flight to reach the man.

The flight crew of an HH-60 Jayhawk helicopter began to plan the medevac mission.

Knowing there would be bad weather along the route, the two pilots entered a series of waypoints in the flight computer. Waypoints are like electronic landmarks. This would help guide the pilots through the mountain passes.

Lieutenant Commander John Turner was the aircraft commander. Lieutenant Jeff McCullars was the copilot. A flight mechanic, a rescue swimmer, and a health services technician were in the back. They would assist in the rescue.

Launching the Mission

The Jayhawk took off at 6:00 P.M. This would be a challenging mission because of the extreme distance. It was dark, so the pilots wore night-vision goggles. According to Lieutenant McCullars, the weather was good when they left Kodiak. The ceiling was at 1,000 feet. Visibility was ten miles, and a light wind was blowing.[1]

The good weather did not last long. A few miles out, the weather got so bad the night-vision goggles were not useful. The winds had picked up, with gusts to twenty-five miles per hour. The ceiling dropped to three hundred feet. But the worst was yet to come.

Farther along the route, the wind increased to almost forty miles per hour, with gusts up to fifty miles per hour. Some aircraft can be dangerous to fly in winds of this speed because of the turbulence. However, the Jayhawk can fly well in winds of over 110 miles per hour.[2] With the snow blowing around them, the visibility along much of the ride was less than one mile. There was constant turbulence; occasionally it was severe. The crosswinds kept trying to push the helicopter sideways. It was difficult for the pilots to stay on course. They could not see, so they relied on their instruments. They used an onboard display on the instrument panel, which shows important information from the aircraft's computers. Some of this information is data from the GPS, radar, and FLIR. These instruments helped the pilots navigate over the many islands along the route.

Near Sand Point, about 350 miles from Kodiak, the sky cleared. The visibility improved, and the crew was relieved to see the nearby mountains. However, the wind

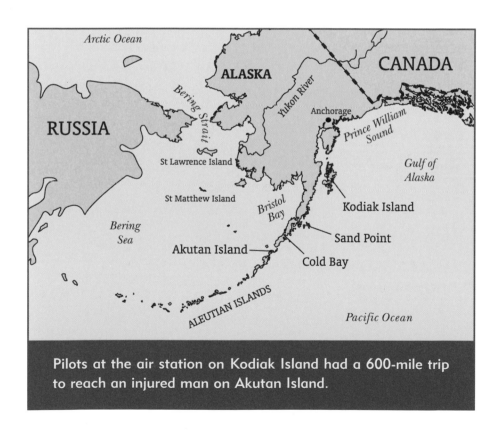

Pilots at the air station on Kodiak Island had a 600-mile trip to reach an injured man on Akutan Island.

increased. The crew was getting tired from the constant turbulence.

They were about 160 miles from Akutan Island when the visibility dropped to less than one mile. The wind gusts were eighty miles per hour. These blizzard-force winds created violent downdrafts. The pilots felt like they were in a falling elevator. Several times the aircraft fell uncontrollably from 300 feet to 150 feet. The airspeed indicator, like a speedometer in a car, bounced wildly. It was almost impossible to read the instruments.

The sturdy Black Hawk helicopter is used in many rescue situations. Here, a specially trained rescue jumper climbs the ladder of a Black Hawk helicopter. He is trained to rescue downed pilots.

Because the flying was so stressful, the pilots took turns handling the chopper. One flew the helicopter while the other watched the instruments, calling out altitude, airspeed, and direction.

The Jayhawk can fly at almost 200 miles per hour, but as McCullars said, "With a direct headwind, we could make only 30 to 40 knots [about 46 miles per hour] over the ground."

Lieutenant Jeff McCullars battled dangerous winds and severe storm conditions to reach the patient on Akutan Island.

When they finally reached the open water near Cold Bay, the winds decreased to gusts of about 25 miles per hour. The visibility increased to about three miles in light snow.

A Stop for Fuel

The crew had traveled about 450 miles, through snowstorms, high winds, and 10,000-foot passes between the mountains. They were almost out of fuel. The nearest airport was at Cold Bay. Four hours after they had taken off from Kodiak, they landed at Cold Bay airport.

After landing, they shut down the engines and waited for the fuel truck. The pilots planned the second leg of the flight.

Because of the extreme cold, the crew could not get the fuel truck pump to work. The pilots had to restart the helicopter and taxi to the in-ground fuel pit. The pit was buried beneath the ice and snow. Again, the crew went outside in the freezing temperature—⁻20 degrees Fahrenheit—to refuel the helicopter. They tried several times but could not get the fuel pit pump to work, either. The clock was ticking. Time was running out for the injured man. One of the crew suggested pouring hot water over the fuel pump assembly. His suggestion worked, and they were able to refuel the helicopter.

"Approximately ten minutes after takeoff from Cold Bay, both of the aircraft's TDPs [tactical data processors]

Rescues in severe weather require special equipment. This C-130 takes off from the frozen snow in Antarctica with the help of skis over its wheels.

failed while we were navigating through a heavy snow shower," said McCullars.

The TDP gathers information from the GPS, the air speed instruments, and the radar. It tells the plane which direction to fly, the distance to the destination, and the wind speed. A loss of both TDPs causes a complete navigational failure. The Jayhawk pilots were flying blindly. Turner turned toward Cold Bay Airport, careful to avoid the nearby mountains. Using night-vision goggles, he was able to pick up the faint lights of Cold Bay. He turned the helicopter toward the lights. McCullars tried to fix the problem by performing several tests. Finally, after he reset the system, the TDPs began working. They turned around again and headed for Akutan Island.

Safe Arrival

Seven hours after leaving Kodiak Island, the helicopter was over Akutan Island.[3] The village on Akutan had no runway, so the pilots had to land in a small field. The high winds, severe turbulence, and freezing conditions would make the landing dangerous. The downwash from the helicopter's rotor was churning up the snow. The pilots worried that a whiteout would prevent them from seeing the ground. The blowing snow and darkness left no room for a mistake.

The crew in the back would act as the pilot's eyes. They would look out the windows and call out any obstacles on the right or left side of the helicopter or near the tail rotor. Turner decided McCullars would land the helicopter. McCullars had a better view of the landing area from his right-hand seat. The crew called out precise instructions to the pilots. This was necessary to get the helicopter in a safe position for landing. Suddenly, the crew lost all visibility in the blowing snow. McCullars slowly lowered the helicopter. Everyone hoped there were no trees below. The last thirty feet seemed to take forever. There was a gentle jolt. The helicopter touched down safely.

Once on the ground, the crew members left the helicopter to examine the injured man. He had a skull fracture and several broken facial bones. He was still bleeding in spite of the bandages the village doctor had applied. He was too sick to move to the stretcher on the helicopter, so they decided to leave him in the temporary stretcher. Several villagers helped load the patient into the helicopter.

≡ Takeoff

The takeoff proved to be as dangerous as the landing. Again, the crew in the back provided lookout calls to clear the trees.

En route to Cold Bay, about 150 miles away, the flight crew worked on the bleeding man. They tried to make him as comfortable as possible.

After arriving in Cold Bay, the injured man was transferred to another aircraft for the flight to an Anchorage hospital.

The flight crew rested overnight. Refreshed, they flew

the helicopter back to Kodiak Island the next day. The crew was awarded Air Medals for their heroism.

Helicopters and fixed-wing aircraft rescue civilians who have been stranded by floods or hurricanes. They also fly injured people to hospitals. Rescue aircraft crews are very brave and often risk their lives on very dangerous missions to save people.

Chapter Notes

Chapter 1. Pilot Down

1. Scott O'Grady, with Jeff Coplon, *Return with Honor* (New York: Doubleday, 1995), p. 28.

2. Celestine Bohlen, "No 'Rambo' and Six Days on the Run," *The New York Times*, June 11, 1995, p. 14.

3. Scott O'Grady, with Michael French, *Basher Five-Two: The True Story of F-16 Fighter Pilot Captain Scott O'Grady* (New York: Bantam Doubleday Dell Books, 1997), p. 54.

Chapter 2. Rescued from the Enemy

1. Jennifer and Jim Stolpa, "Survival," *People*, March 15–22, 1999, p. 224.

2. Scott O'Grady, with Michael French, *Basher Five-Two: The True Story of F-16 Fighter Pilot Captain Scott O'Grady* (New York: Bantam Doubleday Dell Books, 1997), p. 109.

3. Ibid.

Chapter 3. Lifeguard Flights and Rescue Aircraft

1. Andrea Kannapell, "Look, Up in the Air," *The New York Times*, September 27, 1998, p. 4.

2. U.S. Army, *Technical Operations Manual, TM 1-1250-237-10, Change 5*, October 31, 1996, pp. 2–55.

3. Lieutenant Jeff McCullars, Statement for UCN-234 "M/V ME-TOO" and "CAN-TOO," U.S. Coast Guard, September 7, 1998 .

4. Dr. Jerri Nielsen, with Maryanne Vollers, *Ice Bound* (New York: Hyperion, 2001), p. 349.

5. Joe S. Isom, "Mayday! Mayday! Fishing Vessel *Gannett*, 139054/44016.3," *Customs Today*, Department of the Treasury, Summer 1994, p. 18.

6. Ibid.

7. Avflash, vol. 7, Issue 28b, July 12, 2001, <www.Avweb.com>.

Chapter 4. Medevac Equipment and Crew Training

1. Witnessed by the author on a rural Georgia road in 1995.

2. Paul Proctor, "Fire-Fighting Fleet Stretched to Limit as U.S. West Burns," *Aviation Week & Space Technology*, August 21, 2000, p. 38.

3. Bayflite, "Bayflite Air Medical Transport: Saving Lives at the Speed of Flight," 2001, <http://www.bayflite.com>.

4. Author interview with Tammy Gonzales, April 9, 2001.

5. Doug Payne, "When Time Counts: Life Flight Has Put Many a Trauma Victim on the Road to Recovery, Thanks to Fast Helicopter Crews," *The Atlanta Constitution*, July 6, 2000, p. B-1.

6. Gonzales.

Chapter 5. Rescue in Alaska

1. Lieutenant Jeff McCullars, "Summary of Action UCN-58 Akutan Medevac, December 27–28, 1997," U.S. Coast Guard.

2. Author correspondence with Lieutenant Jeff McCullars, May 7, 2001.

3. Author correspondence with Lieutenant Jeff McCullars, March 3, 2001.

Glossary

call sign—The name a pilot uses when flying.

ceiling—The distance between the ground and the bottom of the clouds.

downdraft—A strong downward rush of air.

downwash—A wind formed beneath operating rotor blades.

FLIR—Forward-looking infrared sensor. FLIR detects the heat from an animal or from an aircraft's body and engine, and displays it on a monitor.

GPS—Global Positioning System. A network of U.S. satellites that transmits radio signals for navigation.

hover—To stay in the air without moving in any direction.

main rotor—The large rotor on top of a helicopter that lifts it into the air.

Mayday—An emergency call for help from a ship or an airplane.

medevac—Medical evacuation. The mission that flies a sick or injured person to a hospital.

standby—The status of a helicopter when it is ready to fly on short notice.

tail rotor—A small rotor on the tail of most helicopters that keeps the body of the plane from spinning around.

Further Reading

Books

Barrett, Thomas Beard. *Wonderful Flying Machines: A History of U.S. Coast Guard Helicopters*. Annapolis, Md.: Naval Institute Press, 1996.

Chant, Christopher. *Military Aircraft*. Broomall, Pa.: Chelsea House Publishers, 1999.

Dorr, Robert. *U.S. Coast Guard Aviation*. Osceola, Wis.: MBI Publishing Company, 1992.

Jarrett, Philip. *Ultimate Aircraft*. New York: Dorling Kindersley Publishing, Inc., 2000.

Maynard, Christopher. *Aircraft*. Minneapolis, Minn.: The Lerner Publishing Group, 1999.

Schleifer, Jay. *Fighter Planes*. Mankato, Minn.: Capstone Press, Inc., 1996.

Internet Addresses

National Aeronautics and Space Administration. *Off to a Flying Start*. "Introduction to Flight." December 27, 1999. <http://ltp.larc.nasa.gov/flyingstart/module1.html>.

Smithsonian National Air and Space Museum. © 2000. <http://www.nasm.edu>.

United States Department of Transportation. *U.S. Coast Guard*. March 15, 2001. <http://www.uscg.mil/uscg.shtm>.

U.S. Air Force. *Air Force Link*. n.d. <http://www.af.mil>.

Index